MY FELONIOUS FRIENDS

To Jo Anne & Ken

from Nira Butterworth

ALSO BY MIRIAM BROOKS BUTTERWORTH

Celebrate! West Hartford
(an illustrated history, co-authored)

Just Say Yes (a memoir)

My Felonious Friends

Miriam Brooks Butterworth

Antrim House
Simsbury, Connecticut

ISBN: 978-1-936482-79-5

Library of Congress Control Number: 2015931975

First edition, 2015

Printed and bound by Mira Digital Publishing

Book design by Rennie McQuilkin

Front cover and p. iii artwork ("Shattered Self-Image" by
Pierlette Jones) and "Me, Pictures of Thoughts and Actions
that Define Past, Present and Future" by Edward VanEpps
(page 37) are courtesy of the artists and the Community
Partners in Action Prison Arts Program.

Photographs by the author

Antrim House
860.217.0023
AntrimHouse@comcast.net
www.AntrimHouseBooks.com
21 Goodrich Road, Simsbury, CT 06070

*To Oliver, always a partner
and supporter of my undertakings*

*and with appreciation for the use of material from
the Connecticut Partners in Action Prison Arts Program
and special thanks to Ruth Sovronsky
of the Connecticut Civil Liberties Union,
who always knew where to find the information I needed.*

TABLE OF CONTENTS

My Felonious Friends

The author and her husband, Oliver ("Bud") Butterworth

PART I

For several decades beginning in 1956, my husband, Oliver, and I were involved with the Connecticut prison system and some of its inmates as well as with a few criminals from other places. By describing what we discovered about the lives, in and out of prison, of our "felonious friends" and what I learned as a member of two prison-related organizations, I hope to bring some light into a corner of our society most of us would rather not think about. I am not trying to prove our friends innocent – in fact I think they were all guilty as charged – but rather to show that they, their characters, and their actions were as varied and as complicated as those of us who have never been incarcerated, and that they deserved to be treated humanely, with a chance for rehabilitation and growth.

FELON # I

About fifteen years before we became deeply involved in prison issues, Oliver and I met our first felon. He was a minister and a recidivist. We didn't know him for long, only for a few hours in 1941, when he and his wife came to live for several months in our West Hartford home.

We were moving out. It was the beginning of

a new semester at Kent School, a boys' preparatory school in western Connecticut, where Oliver was teaching. For the first eight years of our marriage, whenever school was in session, we lived in that beautiful Housatonic Valley. Not wanting to leave our West Hartford house empty, we lent it to various friends and acquaintances who needed a roof over their heads. This time it was a young newlywed couple on their way to Bethlehem, Connecticut, where the husband had been offered a job as pastor that would begin in a few months.

Our new house sitter had been sentenced to a prison term for refusing to register for the draft. He was a fervent pacifist and couldn't bring himself to participate in the killing of another human being. He became a recidivist sentenced to another year's imprisonment when he again refused to register after he had served his first sentence.

I remember him particularly because of a delicious story he told about one of his prison experiences. He'd been allowed out in "the yard" for exercise and fresh air when another prisoner started talking with him and asked why he was there. Our friend told his story, and the other prisoner laughed. It was Myer Lansky of Murder, Inc., a notorious killer for hire. "So you're here because you won't kill anybody and I'm here because I will," he said, shaking his head in amusement.

This first friend's story may sound like just

an amusing anecdote, but it brings up a more serious question: What are prisons for? Punishment? Coercion? Protection of society? Rehabilitation?

FELON # 2

The second felon we knew was our doctor.

Parker Dooley was an old friend. He had been a young charismatic doctor for a year at Kent School when my future husband, known as Bud, was a senior there and number two man on the varsity crew. Father Sill, founder and Head Master of the school as well as a highly competitive oarsman himself, was so eager to beat Kent's competitors that he pushed his favorites to their limits. It was inevitable that "Doc" Dooley and "the old man," two forceful personalities, would clash at some time, and that time turned out to be Doc's first and last year at the school. Concerned about the boys' health, Doc countermanded what he considered the Head Master's ill-advised insistence that the crew follow their grueling practices on the river with a mile run around "the triangle," no matter what the weather or the state of the students' health. The boys could see that Doc wouldn't keep his job long, so they dedicated their year book to him.

About eighteen years later, Parker returned to the town of Kent where he began a private prac-

Felon # 2, Parker Dooley, M.D.

tice and became the doctor for the town's elementary school. By that time we had three children, for whom Dr. Dooley became the pediatrician. Although we soon left Kent for West Hartford, he remained our children's twice-a-year doctor and our occasional consultant.

According to our Kent School faculty friends who had known him earlier as a colleague, during the time he was away from Kent Dr. Dooley had worked with Dr. Benjamin Spock and urged him to write his well-known parenting book, my bible as a young parent. And for years he had been head of pediatrics at the University of Chicago's Medical Center. Looking for a new challenge, he left Chicago, planning to set up a practice in Puerto Rico where he hoped to gain a fuller understanding of children from another culture. He stopped by Kent on his way, broke his leg in an accident, and changed his plans.

He spent his recovery with an old friend, Myra Hopson, owner of a large farm on Skiff Mountain. On her farm was a sweet little lake with a cabin on its shore, and there Parker was persuaded to carry on his life's work. Miss Hopson, an older woman, was delighted to have a neighbor who would share the farm and lend a hand when needed. It was there at the cabin as well as at his town office that we knew him when he became our doctor.

So he stayed in Connecticut and, in addition to starting a private practice and becoming the Kent elementary school doctor, he began to treat seriously disturbed children, "incorrigibles," at his cabin on the lake. He took them in one by one when referred to him by desperate parents or colleagues who had given up on them, and he seemed to perform miracles. He never had more than about five at any one time. Each was given very personal, constant attention, especially when they first arrived. I remember two of them.

At one of our bi-yearly visits, when Kate was about one and a half, one of Doc's boys came in to his office and asked if he could take our eight-year-old Michael next door to Casey's, the only store in the village at the time, to buy some candy. Doc looked at me, and I said sure. After they left he said, "Three months ago that boy did $300 worth of damage to a padded cell." I trusted Parker, but you can imagine how relieved I was when the two boys showed up just as promised.

One of the last "incorrigibles" Parker agreed to help was known as the Wolf Cry Boy. Parker, who was beginning to make other plans, reluctantly agreed to take him on, persuaded by desperate parents and the Lakeville clinic where he was a patient and which, by the way, was run by my cousin Rachel. At unpredictable times he would make a loud, wild, ungodly sound. It sent shivers down one's spine. He couldn't control the frequency or the timing or the volume of his outbursts, so of course he couldn't sit in a classroom, take public transportation, or go to a movie or to any other public gathering. Tourette's Syndrome? There weren't any confirming symptoms.

It was about a year and a half later that we took our children abroad for a year and a summer. The story we got from friends when we returned was that Parker had invited the Wolf Cry Boy's brother to visit at the cabin, presumably to find out more about his patient's family. The brother reported to his parents that Dr. Dooley was a "pig," his term for molester, and the family reported that to the police. Parker didn't contest the charge, thus avoiding the need for his vulnerable patients to testify, he said. And that was his path to prison.

By the time we visited him at the dismal state institution in Wethersfield, he had become his fellow prisoners' guru, encouraging inmates to take as much control of their lives as they could, and helping to start a school at the prison that was organized and taught by the prisoners themselves. He also wrote acerbic letters to the Governor and the newspapers about the Wethersfield prison's health services, or lack of them. We gathered the warden was happy to see him leave when he had served his time.

Parker lost his license, of course, along with his voting rights, but desperate parents still consulted him about their problem children. One of the assistant wardens even brought his disturbed son to Dr. Dooley's cabin for help. Another desperate assistant warden lived at the lake with him a while in hopes of curing his alcohol dependency. Parker was paid by a bushel of potatoes or maybe a home-baked apple pie.

About eight years after leaving prison, Dr. Dooley died of pancreatic cancer. The "incurable" boys he had helped were all at his memorial service, including the Wolf Cry Boy, who by then was able to be in public places without erupting in shrieks and had refused to return to his family when Parker went to jail.

My cousin Rachel never forgave Parker, but the town folk evidently did. At least any distrust of Parker didn't brush off on his relatives. Some years later, when Myra Hopson died, Dr. Dooley's nephew, Paul, inherited the farm, lake and cabin and all. He and his wife started a real estate business that was highly successful. For many years, Paul served the town as a well-liked First Selectman, and both Paul and his wife Beth became pillars of the community.

Did Parker really care about the well-being of his patients? I say a very definite "Yes" because of the insightful understanding and effective care he gave to our family and so many others. Once when I was waiting to see him in his town office (I think it was Kate's turn), he left the patients he was seeing to talk with us. As the door opened and closed, I could see a mother with a stricken expression on her face, dressing her year-old twin daughters. Parker was seething. "I'm so glad to have an excuse to get out of that room," he said. "Those little girls have rickets! NO child these days should get rickets!" Evidently the mother had decided the girls didn't need to take the cod liver oil Dr. Dooley had prescribed because she was nursing them and had heard that mother's milk was all they needed!

Did I question whether Parker was guilty? No. Many years before, I had become friends with a young woman named Polly Gunn who had once been engaged to Parker. I knew her for less than a year during my first year at Kent, before we had children or any thought of needing a pediatrician. She and I occasionally climbed the surrounding mountains together and swam in one of Kent's mountain lakes. She told me she had broken off her engagement with Parker when she found him in bed with a couple of young boys.

As I'm writing this, it isn't Parker Dooley's psychology I'm confused about, but rather my own. Why did we take our children to him when we knew all that we did about him? Why didn't we disown him as a friend when we knew what he had done? Perhaps it was a belief that there is often good in people who do bad things and suspect there's also a possibility of bad in the best of us? Perhaps in the '50s we didn't fully appreciate how damaged children can be by sexual abuse? Our children liked him too. Whatever the cause of our tolerance, we stayed friends with Parker.

He also inroduced us to another felonious friend. At the end of our visit with him in prison, he said, "I have lots of visitors, but some of the men here don't have any. Instead of coming to see me, how would you like to become a visitor for somebody else? I'll pick a prisoner for you who hasn't been so damaged that he can't relate."

So that is how we became good friends with Herb Brown and grew to know other prisoners and what happens inside those prison walls; how we eventually became a part of the Prison Association and Families in Crises; how Bud was commissioned to write a book for children with parents in prison; and even how I came to think we might find some good ideas in Nicaragua's idealistic and revolutionary methods of incarceration.

But back to our friendship with Herb Brown, to whom we paid our first visit after he wrote, at Parker's urging, saying how glad he was to hear we were back in town and would we like to visit him. (The initiative had to come from the inmate according to prison rules.)

Unasked, Herb told us he was imprisoned at Wethersfield because he and some "friends" had been caught in an armed robbery. He'd been told that the owner of the house to be burglarized was away and also that no one would care what happened to him or his property, since he was a Communist. Wrong on all counts! When he told us, Herb had a sheepish grin on his face, showing us he'd realized even at the time what a lame excuse that was.

Bud and I visited Herb Brown about once a month for eight years, skipping summers when we were in New Hampshire. We talked to him about our family and whatever was happening in our lives. In return, he told us what was going on in his life at the prison, which by the end of our visits had been moved to more modern buildings in Somers. Herb was easy to like, and we soon found ourselves chatting as if we were old friends.

Entering the prison to visit was never easy and always included a dark feeling of dread. It was painful to sit in the waiting room with parents or wives, trying to ignore their vulnerable look of shame or weary resignation. We somehow felt like imposters, not as rightfully there as the suffering others. It was even harder to watch the children – some out of control and acting out, some hanging on to their mothers as if to make sure they too wouldn't disappear through those big doors. How dangerous was that grim looking guard who watched visitors' every move and tapped the inmates on the shoulder to indicate that visiting hours were over?

On a positive note, a group of Quakers from the Hartford Friends Meeting was given permission to start a day care facility in the new prison that would be open to children during visiting hours. A room was set aside, furnished with donated toys and manned by volunteers. Children could greet their fathers and then be escorted to the play room, letting their parents have a more private visit and relieving the children's feelings of tension. Another advantage – a few of the prisoners qualified as caretakers and were allowed to help with their children.

Here's a more disturbing story. I can't remember the timing, but after Dr. Dooley had left the prison scene, a new warden was hired and a short time after that, one of the prisoners died of bleeding ulcers *in his cell!* The prisoners were outraged. Such an example of negligent health care! At the next meal, many of them protested by refusing to leave their cells. Consternation! Mass disobedience! Who to blame? No one admitted organizing that rebellion, and they couldn't put *all* the men in solitary confinement. There wasn't room. So the administration arbitrarily picked a few (maybe as many as 10) of those they considered leaders to be punished for the whole community. Our friend Herb was one. The warden might have gotten away with his arbitrary move if he had combined it with listening to the prisoners' grievances or had announced a reasonable time when the "leaders" would be returned to their usual cells. Instead the "chosen" were kept in solitary confinement for weeks and weeks. No one was told why those particular ten had been selected for punishment or when or even if they would be released. The action the inmates took had not threatened a riot. It was not that they had refused to return to their cells: they had merely refused to leave. It was a non- violent protest. If the authorities had been afraid of further trouble, they could simply have locked the prisoners in.

While Herb was in solitary, we were still in touch with him, since he was allowed to write. So we were able to track the ebbing of morale and the gradual breaking of the men put in solitary. After well over a month of punishment, some began to trash what they could in their cells, breaking the toilets, for instance, which would be a real reason to discipline them further. At this point we too were outraged, so we called Tom Grasso, husband of our Secretary of State, Ella Grasso, our future governor and a good friend and former classmate of mine at Chaffee School in Windsor. Tom was in charge of the parole department, and we hoped he had enough clout to influence the warden. "It

is more than correction intended when the punishment meted out produces more crime rather
than lessening it," we argued with some emotion.
Fortunately, the men were soon released from solitary and there was no further retribution.

The next time we visited Herb, we naturally
talked about the ordeal he and his friends had
just experienced and marveled that Herb's letters
to us during that stressful episode had not been
censored – or ours to him for that matter. While
musing about what we could do if that should
happen in the future, Bud jokingly described a
trick Boy Scouts were taught. The person being
held for ransom, or whatever the imagined story, would write a bland letter to some hoped-for
rescuer and between the lines would write an ur-
gent message in milk. When the milk dried the
message disappeared. If the recipient expected
a secret message, he would put the letter under
some heat and the milk would stand out in very
readable brown – if you didn't burn the paper up
in the process. Herb was tickled with the idea of
fooling the censors and said he would try it. Sure
enough, the next letter we received from him we
put in our toaster oven and – voila – there was his
secret message (nothing that really needed to be
hidden) emerging between the lines of his normal
correspondence.

Now for a happier episode. Toward the end
of our prison visits to Herb, we were allowed to

attend a graduation of the school that the inmates had started, and we actually sat next to Herb in the audience. Awards were given out at the same ceremony. For instance, one prisoner was given an award for Best Behaved Prisoner of the Year. Herb told us the recipient had murdered his wife in a moment of passion when he returned early from a business trip and found her in bed with another man. We watched the model prisoner walk stiffly onto the stage to get his certificate, turning corners with almost military precision, every muscle crying out "Guilty."

We were on the board of the Prison Association by that time and were told that if psychopathic serial killers were not counted, murderers had a lower rate of recidivism than any other criminals. Herb introduced us to various other friends of his: a man named Everett from a well-known Boston family, a Harvard graduate who had majored in Greek and Latin. He was busy that night because he was one of the main organizers of the school and its "president." Another of Herb's friends we met was Parker Young from New Haven. These friends of Herb's in later years became our friends too, and in this narrative are labeled Felons # 4 and 5.

Herb was released from Somers around Thanksgiving and was able to celebrate our favorite holiday with us before he had to report to a New York prison. He still had about three more years of a sentence to serve there, since he had violated parole by committing the robbery in Connecticut. We went on our usual Thanksgiving Day walk while the turkey was roasting and then, after the yearly organizing hubbub, we served and sat down to a typical New England holiday dinner. I can't remember who was there besides our family of six, but in those days we always celebrated with my brother's family, which included four boys about the same age as our four children, and a few more relatives and friends. My widowed father was one. There were certainly over 15 of us (maybe as many as twenty). You would think that such a mob of strangers of mixed ages and mixed genders would have unsettled a new parolee, but Herb seemed at ease. After all, these were the characters we had been telling him about for eight years, and I think he felt he knew them. In turn, those gathered treated Herb with their usual casual acceptance of an unusual dinner mate, as if they were used to exotic guests showing up at all hours, which they were.

That was the year Dan, our third son, had decided to dress up our Thanksgiving table with some goblets he'd borrowed from the family of good friends of his. They had been unused for some time, languishing in the cellar, and they were embossed with real gold. Herb's eyes lit up, and once when he knew I was looking, he pretended to swipe one. He smiled at me and I smiled back, as if I knew he was just joking – no worries, much.

The next three years Herb spent in the New York prison marked the end of Herb's prison career, although up to that point he had been the ultimate recidivist. In his late 50s or early 60s, cheerful and personable, he got a job as a super in an apartment building. (How on earth did he get *that* job?) We heard from him almost regularly. He would send me a mother's day card or call us to hear our family news. Some years later, after Bud's death, I got a letter from a woman in California, telling me that Herb had died too. I was pleased he had asked her to let us know and pleased to think that he had spent a substantial number of his adult years living a real life on the outside.

FELON # 4

Remember Mr. Everett, that Harvard Graduate from Boston, the head of the prison school that we met when attending the prison graduation? Malcolm Pitt, who like us was a volunteer prison visitor and a prestigious member of the Hartford Seminary faculty, became good friends with the very likable Mr. Everett, such good friends that in 1959 Everett got out on parole with Malcolm Pitt's sponsorship.

At that point, he needed a job. He had good credentials, being a classical scholar from Harvard and the scion of a renowned family. He was also an affable, self-assured person with an impeccable sponsor.

His first stop with his sponsor was Hartford College for Women. They met with the President, Laura Johnson, and Bud, who had been teaching there for many years and had become Miss Johnson's right hand man. Miss Johnson looked like the Vermont spinster that she was, but she was a great deal more sophisticated than you'd guess at first glance. Bud reported that Everett leaned across the desk and said to Miss J., "You're the first woman I've seen in five years." I got to know him well enough later to know that he liked being provocative and it was obvious prison hadn't broken his antic spirit. He didn't get the job teaching classics at Hartford College that he was seeking, but not because of his cheeky attitude. Truth was that Miss Johnson never hired a person until she knew how well he or she taught, and there had been no opportunity for him to demonstrate his abilities.

But that wasn't to be the last of Mr. Everett. In June of that same year, I graduated from Wesleyan University with a Masters degree in History. Since I had taken no education courses, I was not qualified to teach in the public school system, so I sent my résumé to a few private schools nearby. It was so late in the year, mid-June, that I didn't really expect to find any openings. This was kind of a trial run. But within the week, I had a call from Miss Ferguson, Headmistress of Ethel Walker School. Someone in the History Department had just notified the school that she had become very sick and would be unable to return in the fall. Would I care to take over her two courses, History of the Middle Ages and Ancient History? I knew little about the first and had forgotten most of what I'd once known about the second. My studies at Wesleyan had been in Modern European History with some American History mixed in, but I thought I could wing it. I had a summer to prepare. Later in July, I had another call from Miss Ferguson. This time she said another teacher had called in sick. Could I add a course in Latin to my two History courses? Not a chance! I had flunked high school Latin once, and although I'd made it up the next year, I wasn't going to spend any more of my life studying and teaching about Caesar's bivouacs, troops and strategies. (Apologies to lovers of Latin who reveled in Cicero and Ovid.)

In September, just before school began, the trustees entertained us teachers and staff at a dinner at the Avon Old Farm Inn. A good way to begin the school year and a career! As we were leaving, I said goodbye to Miss Ferguson and added that I hoped she had found someone to teach the Latin courses I had turned down. "Oh yes," she answered with a happy smile. "I've found a man who graduated from Harvard in classics. He's highly recommended by Malcolm Pitt from the Hartford Seminary." At that she turned to say good bye to someone else. Did she know her new hire had just come out of prison? If not, should I say anything about it? Would I be the only one who knew his story? No, no and yes. I talked over my concerns with Miss Johnson, and she pointed out that his MO was no threat to the students or the school. He'd been in prison for forging checks, first going through his mother's estate and then his aunt's. So I was put at ease, and his presence or often lack of it gave my first three months of teaching an extra spice I hadn't expected.

Once a week, our schedules placed Everett and me in adjacent classrooms, and we could hear his class roaring with laughter while we plodded through theocratic questions or Socratic theories. Was he telling them some jail house jokes? Once when we passed in the hall, he looked me up and down and said, "You're looking very chaste today." There's that tease I was getting to expect. But soon, he began to send excuses. His grandmother had died. His car had died. He'd had an accident. I began to wonder how many sick grandmothers he could get away with. And then one day, about three months into the first semester, a policeman showed up at the school to announce that Mr. Everett had violated parole and was back in prison. Surprise and consternation all around – and some relief on my part. He had been living with a teacher he had met, which sounded like a positive arrangement, but he had begun to drink and to forge checks again – on his new girl friend's bank account?

But he kept Ethel Walker School's reputation clean. The newspaper notices quoted him as saying he had been teaching at Hartford College for Women. So *there*, Miss Johnson!

FELON # 5

As I write about Parker Young (yes, another Parker), the next of our felonious friends, I realize that for the first time I am dealing with race. This is sure evidence that the seven felons I am writing about are not a cross-section of the prison population in Connecticut or anywhere else in our country.

Herb Brown would be described as African-American, but his skin was a light brown. As I write about him now, just as was true when we visited him, I almost forget that he would be categorized as black. But Parker's blackness couldn't be ignored. It was very much a defining part of him. I mention this because I think it explains in part why he committed the crimes he did.

Parker #2 was from a respected New Haven

family. His older brother was a prominent lawyer in that city, and his older sister had made it big in Washington D.C. as secretary to the Secretary of HUD. But Parker, the youngest in the family, was a criminal, in and out of prison from a young age. What had gone wrong? He was quite good looking with a rather slight build, certainly bright and good company. His MO was surprising and revealing. His original crime, and one he repeated whenever he got out on parole, was to go into a sleeping woman's bedroom at night, take some trivial item – maybe an alarm clock – and make enough noise to wake the woman up. She would scream and Parker wouldn't get far before the police caught up with him and put him back in prison. We imagined that Parker was acting out of a deep resentment of racial discrimination and harassment. This pattern had been going on since he was in his late teens, long before we knew him. He was always welcomed back inside because he was very good at running the prison's industrial program, good evidence that he could have made it easily on the outside.

Sometime after we met him at the Somers' graduation and Herb was off to the New York prison, Parker got out on parole. Again he repeated his usual crime and this time he gave the police our name when caught, although we didn't really know him well. We went to the station where he was being held, and there he was, cowering in one of the cells. I had never seen anyone more distraught. He was sobbing, "I didn't do it! I didn't do it!" We ignored what he was saying, indicating that we didn't believe him. Instead we asked him what his options were. He eventually calmed down and told us his biggest fear was being declared "incorrigible," given his long history of recidivism and a new law (Three Strikes and You're Out) that would mean much harsher treatment for his multiple convictions and a longer sentence than he had usually been given. It would also have given him much less of a chance for parole. We promised we would do what we could to see he avoided that fate, and we did manage to help him that much.

The next time he was out on parole was even more dramatic. It was just before Thanksgiving and, like Herb, he spent the day with us. When we went on our usual walk, Parker seemed to know a lot about our neighbors. "Does Kathy Collins still sing?" "The Lampsons have just moved, haven't they?" He obviously had been keeping tabs on our neighborhood. This made us nervous, so we rather hurriedly went back to the turkey and the rest of the family. Later, when we drove him back to the room he was renting in Hartford, he quickly said goodbye, disappeared inside and locked the door. We realized that after years of incarceration, he needed to be locked in to feel safe.

A few nights later, around 11:00 o'clock,

Parker was picked up by a policeman in Wethersfield in front of a movie theatre. He was in the wrong place at the wrong time. What was he, a black man, doing there? Waiting for a taxi. Why there? "I've been at the movies." "But the movies ended quite some time ago." The policeman decided he should take Parker into the station for further questioning. At that moment, another cruiser drove up, and the driver saw Parker drop a piece of paper as he was getting into cruiser # 1. He picked it up and followed the first car to the station, where the first policeman had found that Parker had almost $900 in his pocket. Leaving Parker with policeman #2, #1 went into another room to call Gordon Bates, the very effective and caring Executive Director of the Prison Association of which Bud and I were members, to ask if it was plausible for Parker to legitimately have that much money. Gordon's answer was no, he didn't think so. Gordon then went back to bed but couldn't sleep. Perhaps it was possible. Perhaps the Butterworths had given Parker money that, in addition to the amount the Prison Association gave to all released prisoners at that time, would add up to $900. So Gordon got dressed and went off to the police station to see if he could help.

When Gordon got there, the station was in turmoil and Parker was gone. How could he have escaped two policemen concentrating exclusively on him? Well, the paper that policeman #2 had picked up had listed a Wethersfield address, and policeman #1 had gone back to the next room to call that address. An older woman answered and explained that she was house-sitting for her daughter, who had recently been married and was off on her honeymoon. No, she hadn't heard anything. Upstairs? No. But she'd go upstairs where the wedding presents were to check things out. Policeman #2 left Parker for a minute, having thought of something else to ask the Wethersfield woman, who at that moment was calling back to say that yes, someone had been there and money was missing. Parker grabbed the chance and slipped out.

It was at that embarrassing moment that Gordon arrived. Parker had left behind one piece of evidence, his overcoat, though it was a very cold night. Gordon reported that one of the policemen picked up the coat and felt something crinkle in the hem: another piece of paper which contained the names and addresses of ten newly (or about to be) weds. First on the list was the Wethersfield couple Parker had just robbed and the second, believe it or not, was that of policeman #2, who had just lost his quarry!

Bud and I took a rather perverse pleasure in the situation because this crime didn't follow the same pattern as Parker's previous ones. This time his actions were more "normal." No waking of frightened women. No waiting around to be caught – just a plain old robbery. Perhaps he was getting over his racial resentments?

Parker was gone for almost a year. He was found leading a protest march in New York City and sent back to Somers, where he served his time. Following his release he married a college professor he had fallen in love with during his year "on the lam."

He kept in touch with us, mainly at Christmas time. Once he paid us a visit, and over lunch we caught up with things going on in his life (all good). He left us that day to spend the afternoon with Tom Grasso, who had been his parole officer and had also become a friend. Parker was easy to like. He never committed another robbery, as far as we know. Some years later, we had a letter from his wife, telling us that Parker had died. She mourned him deeply but told us that she and Parker had enjoyed ten glorious years together. How is *that* for a satisfactory ending!

PART II

WHO CARES

It turns out quite a few people and groups of people do care. First, of course, are the families of prisoners whose lives are broken when a parent or offspring or sibling is convicted of a crime: there is shame, fear of what may happen in prison and what may happen to those left behind, fear of the future, resentment (has justice been done and done fairly?), and often hopelessness.

Then there are people and organizations who want to lower the recidivist rate and even help save some wasted lives. Bud and I joined two of these organizations and served on them in various guises for many years. As mentioned above, we first joined the Connecticut Prison Association (CPA), now called Community Partners in Action. At first, that organization, which goes back to 1875, seemed hopelessly ineffective. As I remember, we raised money to give each released or paroled prisoner $5.00 and an overcoat, and we prayed. Period. During the twenty years we were connected with that organization, we saw significant changes, and there have been many more in the forty-plus years since. For us, the high water mark of the Association was the period of time when Gordon Bates was its executive director. Currently, he is writing a history of the CPA, I'm pleased to hear.

Gordon Bates

The CPA today works on a wide number of programs that are aimed at alternatives to incarceration or at easing prisoners' reentry into society in the hopes of reducing recidivism. It provides some pre-trial services and employment support, treats addictive disorders, and offers therapies of various kinds. The CPA also provides some transitional housing for women, some resettlement services, and has a work release program. There are never enough such programs to satisfy the needs of a swollen prison population, but it's a start.

As for programs offered within various prisons, creative and educational ones seem especially effective. A good example is the school whose graduation we attended, of which Mr. Everett was a part. It gave prisoners something positive to work on and gave the prison management a more satisfied community. The CPA started an art program while we were still on the board. The 2014 36th Annual Show of art work from Connecticut prisons featured over 600 artworks from 168 artists, and the talent exhibited was remarkable, as seen below and on the front cover.

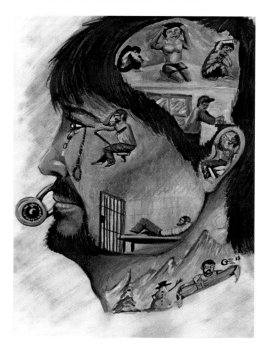

Edward VanEpps: "Me, Pictures of Thoughts and Actions that Define Past, Present and Future"

Some churches and other community organizations also have programs that help prisoners survive incarceration, keep in touch with their families, and get prepared to reenter society. However, the mass incarceration that began in the mid '70s and which has filled our prisons and jails to overflowing has dwarfed the progress that otherwise might have been made.

REHABILITATION OR PUNISHMENT?

In the last half century the U.S. prison population has quadrupled and is up to 10 times the incarceration rate of other democracies. We've seen long mandatory sentencing. The Three Strikes Law requires a life sentence for three convictions, no matter how trivial the crimes. There have been "zero tolerance" laws and lengthy sentences for non-violent crimes – often connected with the "war on drugs". This "war" has been notoriously ineffective, unfairly implemented, and destructive of many lives. Get caught with a little marijuana and it's the hoosegow for you – depending on which side of town you're from. New York and other cities have adopted a policy called "Broken Windows" which means arrests and long sentences for minor crimes. "Catch 'em in the bud." In other countries, prison is a last resort. During this period of emphasis on punishment in the U.S., imprisonment has often been the first resort.

The harmful consequences of a prison record on the life of an ex-convict are hard to overstate. Recidivism is an obvious result. As many as two-thirds of those on parole or who have done their time return to prison, and the costs to society are becoming unbearable, more than a quarter-trillion per year, if all peripheral costs are figured in. We have also seen the creation of a dysfunctional section of society, a dangerous development.

RACE

Race plays a large part in the prison story – in sentencing disparities, stop and frisk actions, inequality in the ability to pay for bail or a good lawyer, or being denied bail entirely. In fact, the ways in which racial attitudes corrupt the criminal justice system can't be exaggerated. On a personal note, my obviously white, auburn-haired daughter, Kate, married a dark-skinned Mexican whose ancestry was a mixture of Spanish conqueror and American Indian. They came north from Mexico to spend summers with us, and she dreaded crossing the border because of harassment by the U.S. Border Guards. It became a little easier after they had a baby. Could the authorities in Brownsville only imagine an illegitimate relationship between a man and a woman of mixed race until they had

Fernando and Kate with children, author, et al. in Mexico

proof of a more lasting and (in their eyes) lawful connection?

Kate and Fernando came to expect being stopped on the road, particularly when Fernando was driving. I'm talking about Connecticut, where they then lived, not Texas or Missouri. Once a West Hartford policeman aimed his gun at him when Fernando reached in his back pocket to get his license, which the policeman had asked for. Another time they were stopped when Kate was driving and Fernando was in the passenger seat. In spite of Kate's explanation that Fernando was her husband, he was ordered out of the car and ordered to show his papers. How can a society function when there is such fear of each other – and such disrespect?

Once in the 1990s, I went with my daughter, who was then working with the Farm Workers Association, to a session at the Hartford Washington Street Court. She was there to support a client who needed some minor court order. I was astonished at the lack of respect shown by the officials for minorities, whether they were there for some infraction of the law, a domestic problem, or a more serious crime. That day an elegant white couple arrested by an overeager rookie policeman for "lascivious carriage" was also called up. Suddenly everything was very professional. Embarrassment all around! Case dismissed! But everyone else was treated with contempt.

Ferando and Kate in Connecticut

Most disturbing to me is that this appetite for extreme punishment seems to have seeped into our public schools. In some systems, behavior that in the past would have meant a trip to the principal's office now involves police action instead. Have that on your record!

One area crying out for reform is the treatment given adolescents in the courts and prisons. In New York, for instance, children as young as 16 are charged as adults. In that State and others, thousands of youths are incarcerated with hardened criminals – subject to physical and sexual abuse from older inmates AND guards. There are many studies that show teen agers have different social/developmental needs and cognitive capabilities, yet thousands of young people are put into solitary confinement for weeks on end. Sometimes that is for their own actions and sometimes for their protection, but whatever the reason, the result is a feeling of abandonment and doom, often leading to suicide.

MENTAL ILLNESS

In the '60s, there was a concerted effort to close insane asylums, to mainstream as many former asylum inmates as possible, with the promise to find appropriate accommodations for the rest. This was done with much humanitarian rhetoric, but the "appropriate accommodations" never surfaced. Many people who needed special treatment ended on the streets and eventually in prisons, the only places left where they could be out of harm's way. Up to 40% of the inmates in many prisons are mentally ill, and harsh incarceration policies are especially unsuited for their needs.

We now know that some punishments are universally counterproductive. Take solitary confinement, for instance. In the 1830s, Alexis de Tocqueville visited Connecticut's state prison in Wethersfield, declared its use of "the hole" outmoded, and wrote about it in his celebrated *Democracy In America,* yet it was still being used when we started to visit there 130 years later! This penalty is rightly labeled cruel and unusual. Some prisoners have been held in isolation cells for months, even years, although studies and intuition tell us that such treatment results in psychological damage and even insanity. It doesn't rehabilitate; it increases crime and jeopardizes public safety, brings on or intensifies mental illness, and costs significantly more than less stringent measures. The newest addition to the Connecticut prison compound at Somers, the Northern, was built exclusively to house prisoners in isolation – around 350 of them. Thanks to legal challenges from several organizations that believe such punishment is unconstitutional, so far the new Northern has been rarely used except for some temporary cases.

WHO PROFITS?

Then there are jobs and money. There's a whole prison industrial complex made up of for-profit prisons and providers of lucrative services to prisons. Communities that harbor prisons are compensated, and guards have jobs that depend on a flourishing prison population. It's our taxes that pay the exorbitant bills. Still there are many in our society who out of fear or a desire for punishment want to incarcerate as many people (not like them) as possible for as long as possible without asking what would really curb crime or prevent recidivism.

ANY GOOD ALTERNATIVES?

In the 1980s and '90s, while still on the board of the CPA, I traveled to Central America five times to get some idea of what was happening there during that agitated period. On one of the trips, I went with a group to observe some projects sponsored by the American Friends Service Committee (AFSC), an organization that we had been supporting. One day our guide took us to a Nicaraguan prison the Sandinista government had built after winning its war against the Somoza dictatorship. Before the revolution, we were told, there had been no real prisons. Prisoners, if not killed, were warehoused in the National Guard's guard posts. The new government, with revolutionary idealism, studied other countries' policies and decided to implement United Nation guidelines on incarceration, and we had a chance to see how that policy was working. First and most importantly, the clearly stated aim was rehabilitation and reintegration back into society.

At that time, there were three tiers of prisons in Nicaragua – two larger than the others where many members of Somoza's National Guard and other security risks were imprisoned, six medium-sized prisons scattered around the country, and thirteen prison farms – closed, semi-open, and open. In the two big prisons I am sure harsher methods were used. At the open farms, however, there were prisoners' councils that met to discuss discipline issues, educational and economic activities, and production. They grew much of their own food. I have seen records that show recidivism at these open prison farms was 15%, an enviably low rate.

We visited one of the six semi-open institutions. The first thing we saw as we approached the prison was a sign painted on the wall near the entrance, whose English translation was "Learning to read can make you free." The underlying understanding, our guide told us, was that crime can't be dealt with in isolation from social and economic factors which constitute its breeding ground. Capital Punishment had been abolished and, except in dire cases, sentences were limited to no more than thirty years – usually far fewer. The guards inside the prisons didn't carry guns on the theory that they should set a good example!

There were several practices in that prison system that I thought might have relevance to our Connecticut prisons. One was a set system of incentives. Every inmate knew that during the first 10% of a sentence, overnight visitors would be allowed every 45 days, and during the next period, a 48-hour home pass would be issued every three months. At a later period, a prisoner could get work outside, gaining skills and building a record of competence. These privileges depended on cooperation within the prison – taking courses, getting jobs, attending therapy sessions. Such a system would keep the prisoners in touch with their families and their communities while providing a strong incentive for getting help and bettering themselves. In addition, prisoners were encouraged to make and save money by being paid the going wage for the work they did within and outside the prison. This was a way to help prisoners get work experience and contribute to their families' welfare, and was good preparation for reentering society. I brought these ideas back to the next CPA meeting, where they were dismissed with a little snickering, but I believe Connecticut is now experimenting with incentives such as conjugal visits, and rehabilitation programs. A lot more could be done.

Sandanista Prison

Other organizations and individuals interested and active in our criminal justice system are various lawyers, psychologists, civil libertarians, social workers, state budget directors, and educators who know the transformation an education can make. There have been recent developments that show a spreading desire to change our obsession with punishment and revenge. Increasing opposition to the death penalty is an example. Some states – Connecticut is one – have recently abolished it completely, perhaps in response to the Innocent Project, which has proved that a substantial number of convicted and executed prisoners were innocent. Also the disastrous "War on Drugs" seems to be waning; some possession of marijuana is now legal, and drug addiction is beginning to be looked on as a sickness that calls for medical help, not punitive action. Pedophilia is similarly being reassessed! Alternatives to incarceration are sometimes available to nonviolent offenders, drug addicts and those who are mentally ill. Universities and various foundations are conducting significant studies that provide a scientific basis for change, another hopeful sign.

To be sure, there are politicians who still cry "You're soft on crime" or "I'm tougher than anyone else," but so far those ploys don't seem to be working as well as they once did. Studies are being undertaken that give us a better understanding of how juveniles' brains mature and how those of the mentally ill and retarded differ from others. But some still argue for giving harsher sentences to those in poorer communities and in bad family situations than to those in more affluent (generally white) communities for similar crimes, noting that studies show a greater recidivism rate for the poor than for their luckier compatriots! Putting the poor and minorities away longer might make society safer longer, they claim. Think about that for awhile! Also in some states, educational programs which have proved successful in modifying behavior have been dropped – too expensive! Two steps forward, one step back – or the other way around.

The other organization of which Oliver and I were a part was started by Margaret Worthington. She and her husband Bill were good friends of ours from Kent, where he had taught American History. They too had been good friends of Parker Dooley and had visited him in prison. When Bill retired from teaching, they moved to Hartford, where Margaret became a social worker. While doing her job, Margaret recognized the great needs of families with an imprisoned member – maybe a mother or a father imprisoned, put away for many years. Was there value in attending to the needs of the families of those prisoners and therefore helping to keep families together? Could an organization with that aim find ways to encourage more visits from family members? Keep telephone calls affordable? Make it easier to keep in touch, and allow inmates to go home again? Margaret and her friends thought so, and in 1979 they founded Families in Crisis (FIC). It now has offices in Bridgeport, Hartford, New Haven, New London and Waterbury.

FIC works to stabilize families and provides services that help change family dynamics. It recognizes that strong family relationships play an important role in helping families rebuild their lives and released prisoners successfully reenter their communities. Its services include family counseling, intervention group services for domestic violence offenders, parent education, visitor transportation, and counseling services for children of prisoners and their caregivers.

Several years after FIC was founded, Margaret arranged with the Junior League of Hartford to fund a children's book that would encourage children to keep in touch with an incarcerated parent or sibling. FIC already had a children's author on its board, my husband Oliver, and also an idea of what was needed to reassure children of inmates that they could safely keep in touch with their convicted relatives. The result was *A Visit to the Big House*. In the book, Rose and Willy go with their mother to visit their father in prison. They are afraid and aren't sure they want to see their father in a place where bad people are put. I won't reveal more of the plot, in case you get the chance to read the book for yourself.

Oliver's story was translated into a Spanish-English version, half of each page being in English, with the Spanish translation below. In addition, the Connecticut Department of Corrections provided access to inmates for interviews and even sponsored a contest within the prison system to find an illustrator. A Somers inmate won the contest, so his name is right up there with the author's – Vinny Collins, Illustrator – and *Una Visita a la Casa Grande* was added to the title. It looked unpretentious, as if it had been made by a family, and

I liked it. With the Hartford Junior League's help, it was distributed free in schools, churches and social service agencies. In 1993, Houghton Mifflin Company reprinted *A Visit to the Big House* in a more traditional form, professionally illustrated, with no Spanish translation. Although lacking its original creativity, in that form it will probably last.

The original edition of *A Visit to the Big House*

Part III

FELONS OF A DIFFERENT STRIPE

My last two felonious friends were both spies. One served a little more than twenty years, and the other is in prison for life. So here is…

FELON #6

John Downey grew up in New Britain and went to Yale, where he was recruited by the CIA in his senior year. On his first mission, he was shot down over China. Both he and his pilot survived and were incarcerated in different prisons. I became acquainted with John almost thirty years later. He had served twenty years of a life sentence before he was released as a result of the so-called ping pong diplomacy practiced during President Nixon's presidency.

Connecticut's Governor Ella Grasso had been instrumental in the freeing of Downey, by insisting that the Nixon delegation have Downey's release on its agenda. Resuming his life back home, Downey went to law school, became an attorney, and needed a job. Coming to the rescue again, Ella created a position for him as liaison between her and the then Chair of the Public Utilities Control Authority, myself.

We had some interesting talks together, sometimes about his prison experiences, sometimes about his plans for the future. He said that the hardest time for him was the first two years of his prison sentence. Nobody knew where he was and he had nothing to do. Then the International Red Cross was given his name and visited him bearing books. Tolstoy's *War and Peace* was a life saver, he told me. He read it through three times, living in his imagination far away in that romantic society. I understood very well indeed. In my senior year in high school, I too had escaped the mundane present by becoming Tolstoy's Natasha, confronting the complexities of growing up, falling in love, and loving to dance. It's the perfect book to escape into.

He also told about his fears when, some years later, some captured Americans became prison mates and began trying to subvert the system. They smuggled notes into his cell on bits of paper and tried to communicate with him by working out a series of taps. These are standard procedures for prisoners, but John was facing a life sentence that would continue long after the newcomers had left, and he had earned some cherished privileges which he desperately wanted to keep.

John did describe one form of resistance that I never understood. He refused to learn Chinese. And to compound my surprise, by the time I knew him, he had met and married a lovely American

Chinese woman. "Love goeth where it listeth."

In another conversation, John told me he was considering a career in politics by running for the Senate. What did I think of that? How could I diplomatically tell him he didn't stand a chance? He had been out of the public's eye for decades and had not created a political following. Nor had he spent the years fund-raising and creating the kind of political reputation it takes to be nominated by a party. Above all, his twenty years away from changes in the U.S. had created a huge gap in his understanding of our country. Like Rip Van Winkle, any politician who slept through the American '60s couldn't possibly understand the constituents he wanted to represent. Of course, that dream of John's didn't come true, but he was a free man with a nice wife, and that seemed to me to be enough of a miracle for any spy.

John Downey and fellow spy at CIA award ceremony

FELON #7

Then finally there's George Trofimoff.

George is the son of a White Russian couple, members of the Czarist nobility, who had escaped to Germany during the 1917 Russian Revolution. He was born in Berlin and was in school there during the Second World War. Toward the end of that war, at age 15, he and his classmates were drafted into Hitler's army and sent to fight on the Eastern Front. During his first battle, George was captured, along with his whole unit. Fortunately for him, it was late at night and debriefing would have to wait for morning. That gave George and a friend the chance to escape. According to George, his friend was killed, but he got away, much to his relief. If his Russian captors had found out his name, they would have known he was Russian, and in their eyes not just an enemy but a traitor.

After his escape, he walked west across Europe, sometimes sleeping in haystacks and begging for food at farmhouses along the way. Each time he knocked on a door, he had to decide what language he should use, Russian or German. Towards the end of his trek, he stayed for some time with two elderly farm women, who gave him a warm welcome and a feeling of relative safety. As the war ended, however, George again felt vulnerable to the Russians, who also were moving west and already occupied nearby territory. He wanted to get to the American Army for real safety, so he said goodbye to the old ladies and, after a few more close calls, reached the American lines. It had taken him months.

The Americans took him in when they found he could help them as a translator, and he went to Paris with them as the war ended. There, he washed dishes and acted as an informal interpreter whenever he could find a job. In Paris, George soon made contact with the rather large Russian community there, and through them he met up with old friends and eventually with his own family. His reconnection with members of this aristocratic line reawakened pride in his own White Russian ancestry, a pride that may have verged on overconfidence with a soupçon of arrogance.

In Paris he also met Tom Bodine, a Quaker from the Hartford Friends Meeting, who gave him a job and listened to George's great desire to emigrate to America. Tom wrote to the Hartford Meeting, and my kind father-in-law, "Uncle" Paul Butterworth, agreed to sponsor him. George arrived in Hartford on a cold December night in 1947, 20 years old, and lived at first with the Paul Butterworth family. Since we lived next door, we got well acquainted with him and heard his stories. He has a great facility for languages and soon became competent in English. In July of the next year, he joined the U.S. Army. Of course that wasn't what the Quakers who sponsored him had in mind. There was much wringing of hands but eventual reconciliation. George was then 21. He had not made any agreements with his sponsors on how he would live his life, nor had he discussed his beliefs or attitudes with them. It was unconditional acceptance on their part. So we kept in touch with him, followed his career in the army, and were sometimes informed of his domestic life.

WHAT WE KNEW ABOUT GEORGE

George rose quickly in the army. He was sent to Fort Ord and Fort Bragg for training and then, while only 22, was stationed in Frankfurt, Germany, where he worked for awhile interrogating Russian prisoners of war. He became a U.S. citizen and a few years later was made a Second Lieutenant in the U.S. Army Reserves. The Frankfurt experience was good preparation for a job he later had in the '60s when, again stationed in Germany, he was head of NATO's Joint Interrogation Center (JIC), where he screened mail coming in from Russia, steaming open the envelopes and carefully sealing them back together. In that '60s job, he also debriefed Russian defectors while wearing a German uniform. During the cold war, Russian officers and other defecting prestigious Russians felt better giving information to Germans than to

Americans, their country's most ardent enemy at that time. A United States citizen and officer pretending to be a German officer! George evidently felt comfortable in any guise.

What kind of a family man was our friend George? In 1955, at age 28, George married his first wife, Frances. The Paul Butterworths gave him a generous gift of $300. A young man with his wrenching history and a new wife would undoubtedly need a leg up. Imagine their dismay when they heard that most of the money went to buy a *dog*! It was an exotic breed, of course – nothing but the best for George!

George's explanation for the failure of his first marriage (there would be five in all) was that the job as instructor and translator at Fort Bragg was boring. He wanted a more adventurous position, which he found in Counter-Intelligence, where his fluency in French would be useful. Unfortunately, there were no accommodations for wives either at the place of training (Hawaii) or in the country to be "observed" (Laos). Frances could move to Bangkok to be closer to her husband, which she tried for awhile, and George visited her there several times for short periods, but she was too lonely to stay among strangers who spoke a language she couldn't understand. The year-long marriage ended in divorce – on the grounds of desertion.

It's George's mission in Laos that I find most

interesting. He and a partner, Bob, were assigned to a group of American military advisors. The two of them traveled through metropolitan and remote areas "observing", making contact with Montagnards and other tribal groups, presumably to assess the Laotians' use of U.S. assistance. They were at first greeted with enthusiasm and feted wherever they went. However, Laos and Vietnam and the whole Southeast Asian area, having just emerged from Japanese occupation, were adopting various brands of Communism, hoping to avoid a return to colonial status in a French empire or an American. By the end of George's assignment, the work he and Bob were doing began to look suspicious. Perhaps they were really making contact with factions that would be encouraged to fight against the Communist government in an attempt to reinstate another empire – this time American. Their lives threatened, he and Bob made an escape by way of the Philippines, which was more firmly in U.S. control.

The adventure George had in Laos was a counter-intelligence operation and during the '60s, once a year, George stopped by Sunset Farm on his way to – was it Fort Bragg? – to teach a class on counter-intelligence activity, and that is how we kept in touch. The '60s and '70s, you will remember, were years full of upheavals, both at home in a struggle for civil rights and in Indochina, to which an increasing number of American young men were being drafted to fight an unpopular war in Vietnam and neighboring Laos and Cambodia.

Once, in the late '60s, George paid us a surprise visit on his way to his yearly teaching assignment. He walked into our living room dressed in his glamorous whites and found five young men from the Hartford branch of the University of Connecticut sitting around on our livingroom floor. They were getting out an issue of a little newspaper against the Vietnam War, *The Jacobean,* which they distributed to fellow students every week. They typed it up on an old Royal typewriter, mimeographed it in our cellar (an underground press if there ever was one), then collated the several pages in our living room, as they were doing when George appeared. I don't know who was more surprised – the students, who were suddenly introduced to a United State's military friend of ours, or George, who looked puzzled and said, "I didn't expect this. We've been told that the young people in America are all decadent and that they party all the time and don't care about anything else."

In the 1960s, George and his third wife lived together long enough to have three children. And it was during the '60s that George became reacquainted and good friends with his older foster brother, Igor, who had become a Metropolitan in the Russian Orthodox Church. Igor was made Bishop for Munich and lived near George, who was then in charge of the Nuremberg Joint Interrogation Center. The brothers visited each other regularly, and Igor occasionally lent or gave money to his younger brother, who as usual was living beyond his means. George often brought important records in his unlocked briefcase when he visited Igor, who turned out to be a member of the KGB.

We had gradually seen George less frequently, although he came by once when he was on wife number four and mentioned to me that he was unhappy because his children from his previous marriage didn't want to be in touch with him. Another time he showed up in the Philippines to visit Jeannie, the Paul Butterworths' daughter who had married an Episcopalian minister then in charge of a school in Mindinao. My last contact with the Trofimoff saga came in the late '90s by way of a telephone call from Andy Byers, George's neighbor in a Florida community for retired members of the military. He was writing a biography of George titled *The Perfect Spy,* describing his exploits as a spy for the United States. Mr. Byers wanted more information about George's arrival in the United States and his early days in Connecticut. I referred him to Jeannie because she had more information than I concerning George's relations with the Hartford Quakers and the Butterworths. A year or so later, we heard that George had been arrested and charged with spying for the Russians in collaboration with his foster brother, Igor. This made the front pages of our newspapers. George, a Colonel by the end of his service, was the highest ranking U.S. Army officer ever to be indicted and convicted of spying for a foreign country. His Florida neighbor writing his biography changed the title of his upcoming book to *The Imperfect Spy*, and George was sent to prison for life.

One thing we discovered in reports of the U.S. trial was that George and Igor had been arrested in 1995 by German authorities and accused of giving German Army information to the Russians. Their cases were dismissed because the German Statute of Limitation (five years) had expired. After the German trial, why did George with his fifth wife, Jutta, move to America, where there is no Statute of Limitations for espionage? The transcript of his trial in the United States gives some answers. He had always found ways to maneuver out of danger and never thought he'd done anything wrong. His ego was unbounded (did he ever really love anyone other than himself?) and he always needed money. He loved fancy cars and expensive houses and furniture. He entertained his fellow retirees in Florida with the best of wines and foods and was surprised to find he was deeply in debt – about $80,000 on his credit card and a large interest debt on a second mortgage for his

Florida house, which he couldn't pay. Brilliant in languages, he had flunked math. He tried to pay off his debts by bagging groceries at a supermarket before he fell for the offer of money that led to his capture.

That is the last contact we have had except for my sister-in-law, Jeannie. She visited him once a few years after he started serving his sentence when, in need of medical attention, he was sent north to a prison hospital. He spent the time with her denying his guilt in spite of all the evidence, and I'm quite sure he believed in his innocence.

PART IV

So we have a conscientious objecting pastor; a sex-offending, exceptionally talented doctor; an armed robber and a second story man, both going straight; a Harvard classicist forger of checks; and a couple of spies, all of whom do time in overcrowded prisons in a system that can't decide what its purpose is – punishment, rehabilitation or protection. These are just the ones I knew, but they are enough to show that those behind bars are real people with all the dreams and capabilities and needs and weaknesses as those of us on the outside. To be sure, their fellow inmates include large numbers of mentally ill, those "too damaged to relate," those who should be someplace where they can get more appropriate treatment than in a prison institution.

Prisons and the Criminal Justice system that feeds them are where the flaws in our democracy are most vividly exposed. The racial disparities in sentencing and treatment are obvious, as are the disadvantages of the poor. Some of the system is being compared to debtors' prison, although our constitution forbids any such. There are those who are arrested, can't pay bail, lose their jobs, upon release rack up more debts, and land in jail for not being able to pay their bills, even though they might have been innocent of the original accusation. And some juveniles are housed with older and more hardened criminals, even though their crimes might be better described as misdemeanors. The description of treatment of youths at Riker's Island in New York is one horrific example.

Lately there have been many references to our criminal justice problems in mainstream media, which is a good sign that a change is happening. We're talking and listening, and this means we're waking up to the destructive treatment and injustices a sizable number of our fellow citizens experience.

Here are just a few headlines that have come across my desk in the past few months:

END MASS INCARCERATION NOW

JUDGE'S DECISION TO HEAR INMATES' CASE THREATENS PRACTICE OF SOLITARY CONFINEMENT (This is a threat?)

RESTRAINTS LINKED TO 3 DEATHS (at Massachusett's Bridgewater State Hospital, cited for harsh patient care of its mentally ill prisoners)

LAW SUIT CLOSES DEBTORS' PRISON IN ALABAMA

For other headlines, see the back sides of the front and rear covers.

Almost every day there is some article about the injustice of our penal system. We are increasingly better informed. This growing awareness, added to the growing protests of the involved communities that are fed up with the unfairness they experience and whose resentment is boiling over, may bring about a significant change. Financial inequality is one thing, but justice applied unjustly can only continue by actions that undermine democracy. It is in the interests of us all to work for a more just society.

ABOUT THE AUTHOR

At 96, Miriam ("Mims") Butterworth is clear about her priorities and responsibilities: civil liberties cannot be taken for granted, and we who are privileged to live in this country must protect them for future generations.

In 1956 Mims and her late husband, Oliver, volunteered as visitors at the Connecticut State prison facility in Wethersfield. Since then she has been a devoted advocate for prison reform along with other types of progressive change.

A faculty member of the Loomis Chaffee School, Mims was a vocal peace activist during the Vietnam War. She marched on Washington, witnessed the violence perpetrated by police at the 1968 Chicago Convention and, as a member of the People's Delegation, attended the 1971 Paris Peace Talks. Later, she helped organize Connecticut's support for the Freeze Movement aimed at halting the nuclear arms race.

Appointed by Gov. Ella Grasso in 1975, Mims served as Commissioner of the Public Utilities Control Authority, and went on to become acting President of Hartford College for Women. She served on the West Hartford Town Council and in 1984 traveled to Nicaragua as an official observer of the first elections under the new Sandanista government. Between 1988 and 1998, she made four more trips to Central America with the American Friends Service Committee and the Center for Global Education, reporting on conditions in Honduras, Guatemala, Costa Rica, El Salvador and Nicaragua.

This book is set in Garamond Premier Pro, which had its genesis in 1988 when type-designer Robert Slimbach visited the Plantin-Moretus Museum in Antwerp, Belgium, to study its collection of Claude Garamond's metal punches and typefaces. During the mid-fifteen hundreds, Garamond—a Parisian punch-cutter—produced a refined array of book types that combined an unprecedented degree of balance and elegance, for centuries standing as the pinnacle of beauty and practicality in type-founding. Slimbach has created an entirely new interpretation based on Garamond's designs and on compatible italics cut by Robert Granjon, Garamond's contemporary.

To order additional copies of this book
or other Antrim House titles, contact the publisher at

Antrim House
21 Goodrich Rd., Simsbury, CT 06070
860.217.0023, AntrimHouse@comcast.net
or the house website (www.AntrimHouseBooks.com).

•

On the house website
in addition to information on books
you will find sample poems, upcoming events,
and a "seminar room" featuring supplemental biography,
notes, images, poems, reviews, and
writing suggestions.